The Islamic World

Beliefs and civilisations
600 – 1600

Peter Mantin

Head of History, Littlehampton Community School

and

Ruth Mantin

Lecturer in Religious Studies, West Sussex Institute of Higher Education

CAMBRIDGE
UNIVERSITY PRESS

For Michael and Naomi

Published by the Press Syndicate of the University of Cambridge
The Pitt Building, Trumpington Street, Cambridge CB2 1RP
40 West 20th Street, New York, NY 10011-4211, USA
10 Stamford Road, Oakleigh, Victoria 3166, Australia

© Cambridge University Press 1993

First published 1993

Printed in Great Britain at the University Press, Cambridge

A catalogue record for this book is available from the British Library

> **Notice to teachers**
> Many of the sources used in this book have been adapted or abridged from the original.

ISBN 0 521 40609 9

Cover illustration: 'Suleiman and Admiral Barbarossa',
Sonia Halliday Photgraphs.

Illustrations by Sue Shields, Peter Kent, Ranjit Rai Quantrill,
Chris Etheridge, Rodney Sutton.
Maps by Kathy Baxendale
Picture research by Jane Taylor, Callie Kendall.

The authors acknowledge the fact that Muslims express their respect for Muhammad and other prophets with the phrase 'Peace be upon him'. This phrase has not been used throughout the text of this book but no disrespect is intended by its omission.

Acknowledgements
The authors and publisher would like to thank the following for permission to use the illustrations on the following pages:

4, J. Allan Cash Photolibrary; 5, 44, 51, A. F. Kersting; 6t, 10, 22 (inset), 26, 34—35 (background), 48r, 60—1 (background), 61b, all patterns on unit introductions, Christine Osborne/Middle East Pictures; 6b, 14—15, 14 (inset), 17, 24, 46b, 60, 61tl, Peter Sanders Photography; 16, Michael Holford; 20, reproduced by permission of the British Library; 22—23, 44—45, 58—59, The Hutchison Library; 23 (inset), 27t, 36, 37, 39t, 46t, 54l, 55r, Sonia Halliday Photographs; 57, Sonia Halliday and Laura Lushington; 27b, 59l, Werner Forman Archive; 28, 32—33 (ewer, glass beaker), 47, reproduced by courtesy of the Board of Trustees of the Victoria & Albert Museum; 32—33: (elephant design fabric), Lauros-Giraudon/ Musée du Louvre, Paris, (birds design fabric), Giraudon/Basilique Saint Sernin, Toulouse, (ivory casket), Museo Arqueológico Nacional, (all remaining items), reproduced by permission of the Trustees of the British Museum; 34—35 (Samarra), Robert Harding Picture Library; 35r, Edimedia/Bibliothèque Nationale; 39b, 49, Michael Jenner; 45t, Ann & Bury Peerless - Slide Resources and Picture Library; 50, Giraudon/Bibliothèque Nationale; 61tr, David Lomax/Robert Harding Picture Library.

Contents

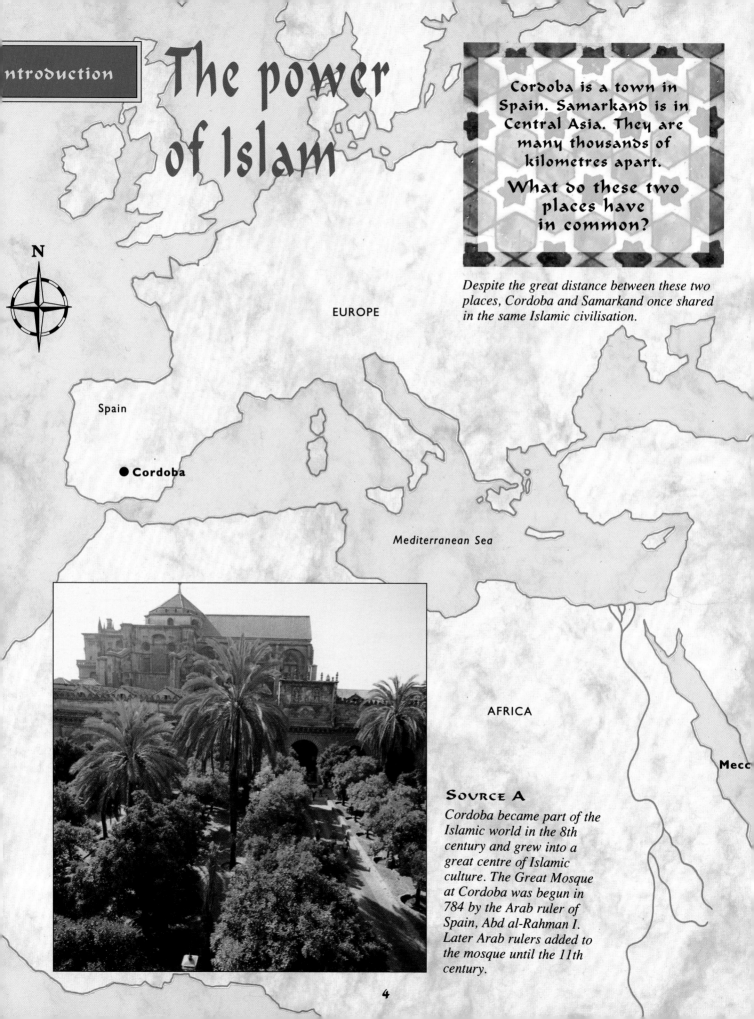

The power of Islam

Cordoba is a town in Spain. Samarkand is in Central Asia. They are many thousands of kilometres apart.

What do these two places have in common?

Despite the great distance between these two places, Cordoba and Samarkand once shared in the same Islamic civilisation.

EUROPE

Spain

● **Cordoba**

Mediterranean Sea

AFRICA

Mecc

SOURCE A
Cordoba became part of the Islamic world in the 8th century and grew into a great centre of Islamic culture. The Great Mosque at Cordoba was begun in 784 by the Arab ruler of Spain, Abd al-Rahman I. Later Arab rulers added to the mosque until the 11th century.

N

4

A new force in the world

In the 7th century a new religious force swept through much of the world. It was called Islam. It has changed millions of lives in past and present times. Islam not only changed people's religious beliefs – politics, language, architecture, warfare, science and many more aspects of life were never the same after the arrival of Islam.

The extent of Islam

Look at Sources A and B. They show Islamic buildings from the Middle Ages. One building is in Cordoba in Spain. The other is in Samarkand in Central Asia. These places are about 8,000 kilometres apart, but they were linked in the Middle Ages by the power of Islam. What was Islam and how did it come to have such an impact on so many people? As you read this book you will begin to find some answers.

This book tries to help us understand:

* the beliefs of a very large group of people worldwide

* where those beliefs came from and why they spread

* different ways of looking at the world

* different points of view about Islam and its history.

ASIA

● **Samarkand**

SOURCE B

A medieval Islamic building still standing in Samarkand, Uzbekistan.

0   500   1000 km

Arabian Sea

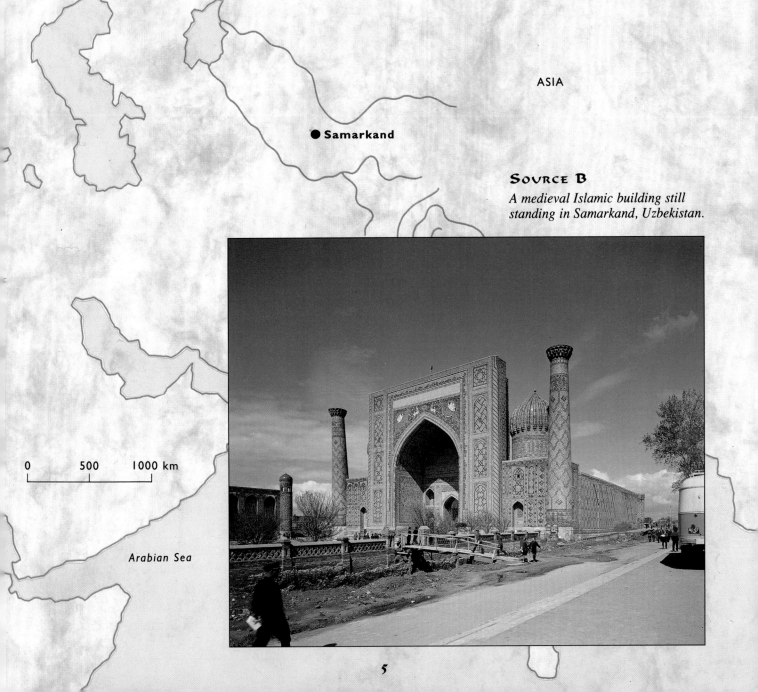

The religion of Islam has had a great influence on the history of human life. Islam today has followers in many countries worldwide and is the fastest growing religion in the world.

The holy city of Mecca, which Muslims call Makkah, is at the heart of the Muslim world. Not all Muslims are Arabs though: in fact Arabs make up only one-sixth of the world's Muslim population.

NORTH AMERICA

SOU

Over 85%

51 — 85%

21 — 50%

6 — 20%

1 — 5%

less than 1%

Muslims praying in a mosque in Pakistan. Wherever Muslims live, and whatever language they speak, they all follow the same rituals of prayer in Arabic.

One God called Allah

Islam is an Arabic word which means 'submission' (to the will of God). People who believe in Islam are called Muslims. Islam teaches that there is only one God, and they call Him Allah. Allah is an Arabic word meaning 'the God'.

Islam?

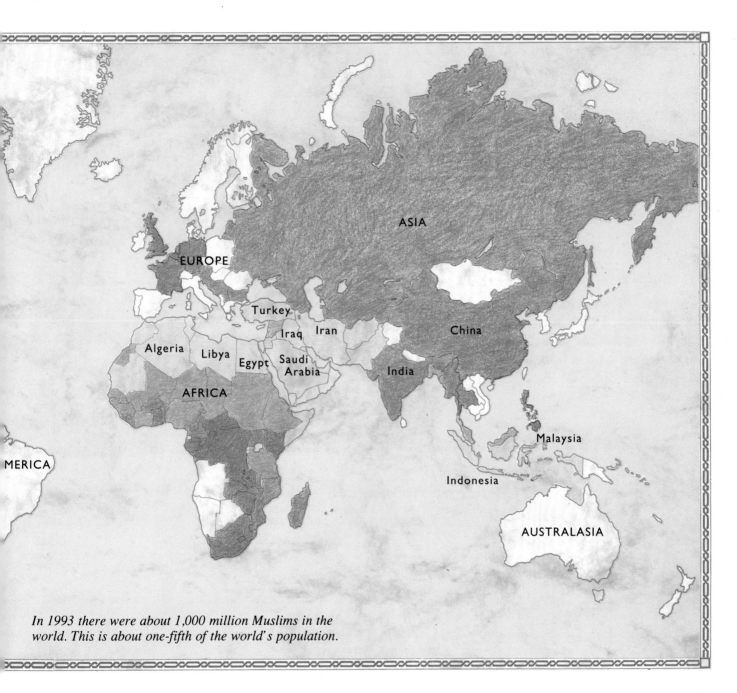

In 1993 there were about 1,000 million Muslims in the world. This is about one-fifth of the world's population.

Muhammad, the Prophet of Allah

The religion of Islam was founded in the country now called Saudi Arabia by the Prophet Muhammad, who lived from about AD 570 to 632. For Muslims the Prophet Muhammad is the first leader of Islam and is their last and greatest Prophet. His story is told in Unit 5.

Who are the Muslims?

If you look at the map you can see that Muslims do not just live in Saudi Arabia. Islam has spread far and wide across many continents. Arabic is the common language of Islam and we shall be investigating the common set of beliefs which unites Muslims everywhere.

7

What do Muslims believe?

Muslims are united in their belief that God's teachings have been revealed through the Prophet Muhammad. By following these teachings Islam offers a complete way of life to all Muslims.

What are the essential Muslim duties?

The five pillars of Islam

Muslims believe they have five main duties. These are known as 'the five pillars of Islam' because they provide support for the Muslim way of life.

1
Shahadah
(to bear witness)
There is one God, Allah, and Muhammad is His Prophet.

2
Prayer
Muslims should pray to Allah five times a day.

3
Zakah
(alms)

A part of what Muslims earn every year should be given to the poor and sick.

4
Fasting

Muslims should fast from dawn to sunset every day of the holy month of Ramadan. Ramadan was the month in which God's teachings began to be revealed to Muhammad.

5
Pilgrimage

Muslims should try to go on a pilgrimage to the holy city of Mecca at least once in a lifetime.

Before prayer Muslims remove their shoes and wash in a special way. They stand on a carpet or prayer mat, facing in the direction of Mecca. They then pray following set movements and words.

Prayer

Muslims pray five times a day. The prayer can take place anywhere, but it follows a fixed pattern, taught by the Prophet Muhammad.

● Why do you think Muslims remove their shoes and wash before praying?

The Quran: the holy book

The Quran is the holy book for all Muslims. Muslims believe that the Quran is the word of God. The messages which Allah gave to the Prophet Muhammad are recorded in this holy book.

Muslims believe that if people follow Allah's teachings, or 'pathway', they can reach complete peace – with God, with each other and with themselves. Muslims believe that everything you need to know to reach peace has been given to men and women by Allah but that there is still a need for human effort.

The Quran must always be stored in a place higher than any other book. Muslims must wash before touching the Quran and nobody should talk or eat while it is being read.

● Why do you think Muslims have these rules about the Quran?

The word *Quran* means recitation – to tell again. Muhammad was 'reciting' God's words. Muslims all over the world try to learn all the words of the Quran. They believe that every word is the word of God. For this reason, copies of the Quran are treated with great respect by Muslims. The Quran is written in Arabic because this is the language in which God's teachings were revealed through Muhammad.

● How can you tell this is a special book?

The Hadith: the sayings and example of the Prophet

Muslims say that the Prophet Muhammad was an ordinary human being, but that he lived his life exactly as Allah told him to. His way of life is therefore the perfect example for everyone to follow.

For this reason, examples of what Muhammad said and did were remembered by his followers and written down. They are known as the *Hadith* and they help Muslims today to understand how to live as Allah would want them to.

Shariah: the pathway

The first followers of Muhammad put together rules or 'laws' known in Islam as the *Shariah*. This means path, or highway, in Arabic. If Muslims follow this pathway it will lead them to peace and Allah.

Islam says that nothing in the world can divide humans from Allah if they follow the pathway. In the West, people often think of rules as making life more strict and difficult, but Muslims believe that the rules which God has given make life easier and more enjoyable.

There is only one God

The most important saying in Islam is that there is only one God. No part of a person's life is separate from God. Enjoying physical things such as food, sleep and pleasure is not wrong, as long as humans do so according to Allah's rules.

SOURCE A

People show their respect for the Quran by trying to learn as much of it as possible by heart, even though Arabic may not be a language they speak.

Muslims today

If we are to get a better picture of Islam, it is important that we ask Muslims about their religion.

A British historian called Richard Tames recently spent a long time talking to Muslims and asking them to explain the importance of Islam. The diagram shows some of the answers they gave.

ISLAM IS NOT JUST A RELIGION: IT IS A WHOLE WAY OF LIFE. IT GIVES YOU ALL YOU NEED TO LEAD A GOOD LIFE.

ISLAM IS FOR EVERYONE – IT DOES NOT MATTER WHAT COUNTRY YOU COME FROM OR WHAT COLOUR YOUR SKIN IS.

ISLAM DOES NOT EXPECT HUMANS TO CHANGE THEIR NATURE. IT ACCEPTS PEOPLE AS THEY ARE AND PROVIDES RULES TO LIVE AS GOD WILLS.

ISLAM IS NOT JUST SET IN THE PAST. IT IS MODERN, UP TO DATE AND GIVES PEOPLE WHAT THEY NEED TODAY

THERE ARE PEOPLE IN THE WEST WHO DO NOT UNDERSTAND ISLAM. SOME PEOPLE IN THE WEST HAVE DELIBERATELY NOT TOLD THE TRUTH ABOUT ISLAM. THIS ALL GOES BACK TO THE TIME, HUNDREDS OF YEARS AGO, WHEN CHRISTIANS FOUGHT AGAINST MUSLIMS IN THE CRUSADES.

These answers are taken from interviews with Muslims by Richard Tames in *Approaches to Islam*, 1989.

THE MOSQUE

A mosque is a Muslim place of worship. Many mosques are covered by a dome and some have tall towers called minarets. Muslims are called to prayer by a man called a muezzin. Mosques come in many different shapes and sizes, but they all share some common features.

INSIDE A MOSQUE

● There are no pictures in a mosque, but mosques can be beautifully decorated with calligraphy, geometrical designs and arabesques.

● In order to allow prayer to take place, there is very little furniture in a mosque. This creates a feeling of space and calm.

● All mosques have a place for washing. To represent their purity before God, Muslims have ablutions before praying. As a sign of respect Muslims remove their shoes before entering the mosque.

● Every mosque has a mark or niche in the wall to indicate the direction of Mecca. This is called the *mihrab*. All worshippers face this direction behind the imam – the leader.

SOURCE B

Prayers in a mosque teach us brotherhood and equality as in a mosque we find people standing shoulder to shoulder whatever their colour, rank, wealth or job. The king may find a labourer standing next to him, a private may be standing next to a general. No worshipper may object to another worshipper standing next to him. All are equal in the house of Allah.

Rashid Ahmad Chaudri, *Mosque; its Importance in the Life of a Muslim*, 1982

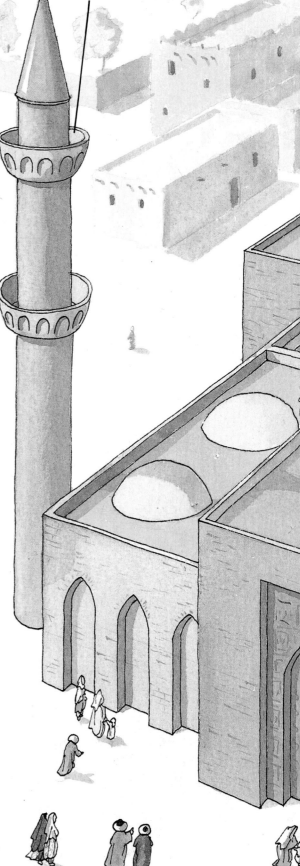

minaret *from which the muezzin calls the people to prayer*

12

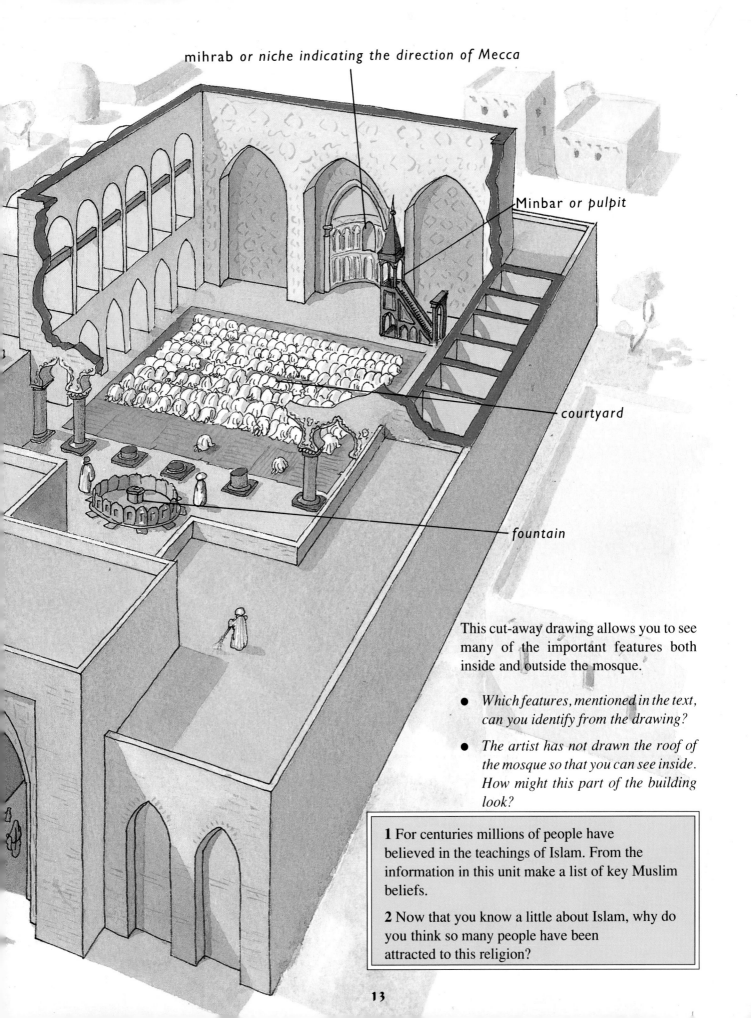

mihrab *or niche indicating the direction of Mecca*

Minbar *or pulpit*

courtyard

fountain

This cut-away drawing allows you to see many of the important features both inside and outside the mosque.

- *Which features, mentioned in the text, can you identify from the drawing?*

- *The artist has not drawn the roof of the mosque so that you can see inside. How might this part of the building look?*

1 For centuries millions of people have believed in the teachings of Islam. From the information in this unit make a list of key Muslim beliefs.

2 Now that you know a little about Islam, why do you think so many people have been attracted to this religion?

13

2 Pilgrimage to Mecca

All Muslims try to travel to Mecca at least once in their lives. These pilgrimages have taken place for many centuries.

How has the pilgrimage to Mecca changed since earliest times?

SOURCE A

The Kaba (or cube, because of its cube shape) at Mecca. It is an ancient stone building covered in a black cloth. It is the most important site for Muslims. Wherever they are, Muslims face the Kaba when they pray.

Pilgrimage of a lifetime

Every Muslim is expected to make a special journey to the holy city of Mecca at least once in a lifetime if possible. This pilgrimage is called *Hajj* and takes place in the same Islamic month each year. Today pilgrims flock to Mecca in their tens of thousands from all over the world. Those who are not Muslims are forbidden to enter the holy city.

Pilgrims in the holy mosque at Mecca.
Pilgrims perform certain rituals during the Hajj such as walking seven times around the Kaba, which they are seen doing here.

Source D

For centuries Muslims have made the special journey to Mecca. Ibn Batutta was a Muslim traveller from Morocco who went on the Hajj in 1325. This is his description of the journey.

'There were so many people there that the earth seemed to move like the sea. With this caravan there were many camels carrying food and water for the poor, and medicine and sugar for those who fell ill. Whenever the caravan stopped, food was cooked in great brass pots, and from these the poorer pilgrims were fed.

There were a number of spare camels for those who could not walk.'

From *The Story of Ibn Battuta*, 14th century

Today the main camp where the pilgrims stay is at the village of Mina, five kilometres outside Mecca. A modern journalist describes the scene.

'For the five days of Hajj the village of Mina houses and feeds nearly two million people. Fly-overs, highways and tunnels under the mountains attempt to ease the traffic jams, aided by a computerised traffic plan. At Mina, Muslims from more than 100 countries live in blocks of tents divided by nationality. Some 22,000 workers clean the camp. Every tent has carpets and either a desert cooker or an air conditioner. Nearby is iced water and toilet facilities. Tens of thousands of poorer pilgrims live in the streets and under the fly-overs.'

From an article by Ahmed Rashid in *The Independent*, 26 June 1991

SOURCE F

The pilgrims' camp at Mina.

1 Sources C and D tell us about the Hajj hundreds of years ago. Source E describes the modern Hajj.

a Explain how things have changed over the years.

b Explain how some things have stayed the same.

2 Do you think that going on the Hajj today is easier or harder than it was hundreds of years ago?

630 Mecca becomes the holy city of Islam

The Prophet Muhammad was born around 570. Muslims believe he was the greatest of God's messengers. He soon had many followers. In 630 the city of Mecca became his headquarters. Muhammad and his followers destroyed the idols and statues they found in the Kaba. Muhammad died in 632.

636 Byzantines defeated at Yarmuk: Syria conquered

In 636 Muslim armies attacked the Byzantine Empire. It was already weakened by long wars against the Persians, so it was a good time for the Muslim armies to attack. Although the capital Constantinople itself was not threatened, many other Byzantine cities fell to Islam.

637 Islam on the march: Persians defeated at Qadisiya

After Muhammad died, his friend Abu Bakr was chosen to be his caliph, or successor. He carried on the work of spreading Islam. When Abu Bakr died in 634, the next caliph was Umar. He led Muslim armies in battle, beating the Persians at the Battle of Qadisiya (which is now part of Iraq). The Persian Empire fell to them in 642.

661 The rise of the Umayyad caliphs

In 661 Muhammad's son-in-law, Ali, was killed. He was the last of the four caliphs who had known the Prophet Muhammad. After this the Umayyad family took control of lands conquered by the Muslim armies. They ruled their empire from Damascus. The Umayyad family continued to conquer many new lands until they lost power in 750.

Islam 600-1600

711 A Muslim army reaches Spain

After the Prophet Muhammad's death in 632, Muslim armies conquered more land in North Africa and Egypt. By 698 they had captured Carthage, which is in modern-day Tunisia. They finally crossed into Europe in 711 and soon conquered most of Spain where they were known as the Moors. Only many centuries later, in 1492, were the Moors finally forced out of Spain.

750 The Abbasid family seizes power

The Abbasids seized power from the Umayyad family, murdering many of them. The Abbasids founded a fabulous new capital city at Baghdad in 762. It became a great centre of learning. The Abbasid Empire stretched from India to the Atlantic Ocean. The fifth Abbasid caliph, Harun al-Rashid, took over the empire in 786. Life in Baghdad during his reign was described in the classic stories of The Thousand and One Nights.

1099 The first Crusaders arrive in Jerusalem

The Abbasid Empire was so huge, and its wealth and power so great, that rivals to the Abbasids began to appear. Christians from Europe took advantage of the rivalries in the Abbasid Empire, and in 1095 Pope Urban II sent Christian armies on a Crusade – a holy war, to capture the city of Jerusalem from the Muslims. The Christians took Jerusalem in 1099; the Mus recaptured it in 1187.

1453 The Ottomans conquer Constantinople

One of the last and greatest of the Islamic empires was the Ottoman Empire which began in Turkey and expanded through the eastern Mediterranean. Power was handed down from one member of the Ottoman family to another, and in 1453 the Byzantine capital, Constantinople, was taken by Sultan Mehmed II. By the time Sultan Suleiman I came to the throne in 1520, the Ottomans controlled a mighty empire. It was to last right up to the early 20th century.

The spread of Islam

Within just a hundred years of the death of Muhammad, Islam had spread over a vast area. The maps show how Islamic rule spread from the time of Muhammad.

How much of the world became part of the lands of Islam in this short period?

Jihad

Jihad is an Arabic word which means 'struggle' – the struggle against evil and God's enemies. (Holy war is known as 'the lesser jihad'– the 'greater jihad' is the struggle with evil within oneself.) The Quran says that believers should be ready to go to war against the enemies of Islam as a last resort, but that they should not be the aggressors. Those killed fighting in defence of Islam would be rewarded by God in the next life. Muhammad set an example of Jihad by defending his followers and leading them into battle for eight years until 630 when he conquered Mecca.

By the time of Muhammad's death in 632, almost the whole of Arabia had been converted to Islam. Muslim traders, travellers and missionaries spread Muhammad's teaching through much of Africa, Asia and Europe. Often this happened peacefully but there was also conflict and his followers began an amazing series of conquests in the Middle East and beyond.

In 638 the Muslims conquered Jerusalem; Jews, Christians and Muslims have fought for control of this city ever since. Within a few years the Muslims had created a huge empire stretching from modern Iran to Egypt and much of North Africa. Islam almost reached Britain: by 720 the whole of Spain had been taken and in 732 the Muslim soldiers reached Poitiers, deep in France, where they were defeated. Belief that God was on their side because they were fighting a holy war was an important part of the success of the armies of Islam.

SOURCE A
Arab soldiers mounted on camels.

1 Use the maps in this unit and an atlas to make a list of modern countries that were, at least in part, Islamic
a before 632
b between 632 and 661
c between 661 and 750

2 Explain in your own words how much the Islamic Empire changed between 632 and 750.

3 Give reasons why you think Jihad was such an important part of the spread of Islam.

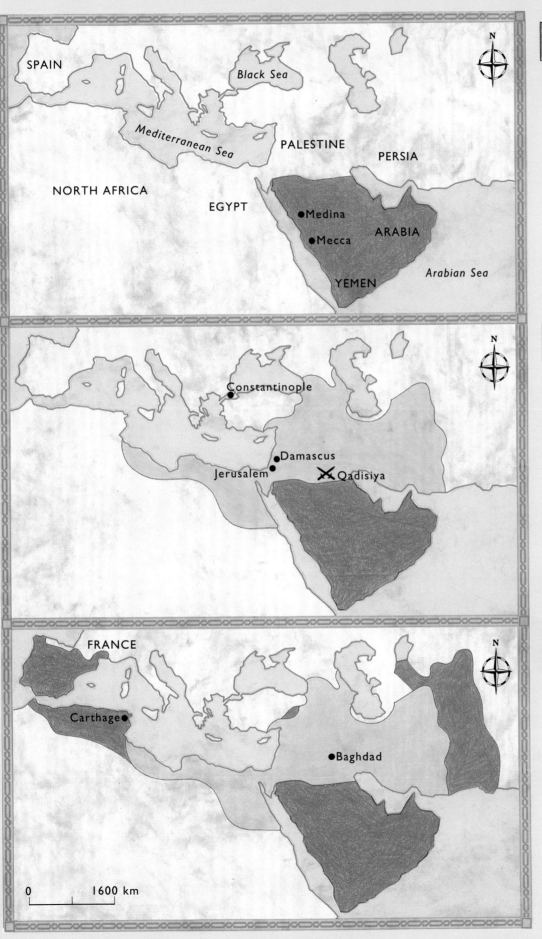

Islamic expansion
before the death
of Muhammad in 632

Islamic expansion
under the first four
caliphs 632–661

Islamic expansion
under the Umayyads
661–750

*The spread of
Islamic rule,
632–750*

SPAIN

Black Sea

Mediterranean Sea

PALESTINE

PERSIA

NORTH AFRICA

EGYPT

ARABIA

●Medina

●Mecca

YEMEN

Arabian Sea

Constantinople ●

●Damascus

Jerusalem●

✕✕Qadisiya

FRANCE

Carthage●

●Baghdad

0   1600 km

4 Arabia at the time of Muhammad

The Islamic religion began in Arabia.

How much do we know about this place in the 7th century? Are there any clues to explain why a new religion should start there?

SOURCE A
Modern bedouin and their tents. Some Arabs still live like this today although others live in modern cities.

A modern caravan of camels in Niger, West Africa. Caravans have followed the same routes for hundreds of years. Camels are able to travel for several days without water.

A desert land

In Arabia, the land is mostly desert. The people have never grown many crops; they have always had to be on the move, looking for patches of grass to feed their flocks of goats and sheep.

Living as nomads

People who move from place to place to find pasture and food are called nomads. Many of the people who lived in Arabia at the time of Muhammad led a nomadic life. The Arabic word for nomads is *bedouin*. These people wandered in search of water and grazing for their camels, horses, sheep and goats. They lived on dates and goats' milk. Camels were used for transport. The meat, milk, skin, hair and dung of the camel were all useful to the bedouin.

- How do you think the lifestyle of a nomad may help spread ideas over a large area?

- How are the bedouin's clothes and shelter suited to the climate and the wandering life? Certain skills were needed to survive in this desert climate. Can you think what they were?

Arabia and surrounding countries at the time of Muhammad. He was born around 570 in the trading city of Mecca.

Towns and traders

Not all Arabs in the 7th century were nomads. Some were traders. They travelled in long lines, or caravans, of camels across the desert, carrying their goods for trade. They brought all kinds of goods, such as spices, fruits and precious metals. Mecca was an important town for trade, and many caravans stopped here.

Worshipping many gods

Mecca was an important religious centre, long before the time of Muhammad. It contained a very old shrine known as the Kaba or 'cube'. The Kaba was believed to have been built by Adam, the first man. At the time of Muhammad the Kaba contained more than 360 statues of different gods, altars and various symbolic objects like meteorites, pillars and slabs of rock. At that time people worshipped many different gods. Some worshipped the sun, others worshipped the planets. Many people carried lucky charms to protect themselves against evil spirits.

SOURCE B

A pre-Islamic stone idol. Idols like this were worshipped as gods, or as symbols of gods, before people turned to Islam.

---

1 Why were many Arabs nomads? Describe the way of life of a nomad living at the time of Muhammad.

2 What can you tell from this unit about the religious ideas of the Arabs before Islam?

3 Look back through this unit. How did trade and the nomadic life help spread new ideas in Arabia?

Muhammad and the early converts

Muhammad was born around 570 in the trading city of Mecca. Before he died in 632 he had changed the lives of many people.

Who was Muhammad?

An orphan boy

Muhammad was born into a noble tribe called the Quraysh. His father died before he was born, and his mother died when he was young. As an orphan he was looked after by his grandfather and, when he died, by his uncle who was a merchant. Later he became a trader for a rich widow called Khadijah, working as the leader of her caravans. When Muhammad was 25 he married Khadijah.

We have seen that most people in Arabia believed in different gods and worshipped stone statues. Muhammad was troubled by this and also by their behaviour. Muhammad did not like the drunkenness and gambling in Mecca, and the fact that women and children were sometimes badly treated.

The moment of revelation

According to Islamic teaching, the word of God was revealed to Muhammad in the year 610, when he was 40. He was sitting in a cave on Mount Hira, near Mecca, when God spoke to him through Gabriel. These revelations happened again and again. In the year 613 Muhammad told people in Mecca that there was only one God, and that God had created the world and everything in it. Since there was only one God it was wrong to worship statues and different gods.

An uphill struggle

At first there was a lot of opposition to Muhammad. His followers were beaten by people who did not want to give up their old way of life. Many people did not like his teachings that duty to God, or Allah, was more important than family or tribe. They persecuted his followers for their new faith.

In 622 Muhammad left Mecca to get away from his enemies. He was invited to go and live with people in the town of Medina, about 400 km away. His departure, or *hijrah*, was important because it was at Medina that Muhammad set up the first Islamic community. Muslims begin their calendar from this date, the first year of the hijrah. The Islamic calendar therefore reads AH 1 when the Christian calendar reads AD 622.

The tide turns

In Medina, Muhammad was in a better position to teach Islam. Many different sorts of people came to Medina to be with Muhammad. There were rich and poor, men and women, nomads, traders and slaves. Muhammad could now lead people in the ways of Islam. A very small mosque (a place to worship God) was built. Later mosques were based on this first mosque – even though many of them are in fact much bigger and more magnificently decorated.

The conquest of Mecca

Battles took place between the Muslims and the people of Mecca. In 630 the Meccans were beaten. Muhammad came back to his home town. The idols were taken from the famous shrine, the Kaba, and destroyed. Now the Kaba is the most important place of pilgrimage for Muslims.

The death of the Prophet

Islam spread very quickly all over Arabia. In 632 Muhammad suddenly fell ill and died. He was buried in Medina. Later, a magnificent mosque was built on the site of Muhammad's tomb (Source A).

◀ SOURCE A

The Mosque of the Prophet in Medina stands on the site where the Prophet Muhammad built the first mosque after the hijrah in 622. From the 7th to the 20th century the mosque has been rebuilt and extended. The green dome was built over the Prophet's tomb during the Ottoman period.

---

1 a Show the main events mentioned in this unit in the form of a timeline.
b Mark on your timeline the period from which the Islamic calendar begins.
c In which year of the Islamic calendar did Muhammad die?
d Why are the letters BC and AD not suitable in an Islamic calendar? What does AH stand for?

2 Explain in your own words some of the problems that Muhammad encountered in his life.

The collapse of the old empires

Soon after the death of the Prophet Muhammad in 632, the Islamic world expanded dramatically. The Muslims defeated the armies of two powerful empires: the Persian Empire and the Byzantine Empire.

Why were the followers of Muhammad able to defeat these two great empires?

The caliphs

When Muhammad died his successors carried on the work of spreading Islam. These leaders of the Islamic community were called *caliphs*. The word *caliph* means 'successor'. They were the successors of the Prophet as leaders of the Muslim community. The first four caliphs had all known the Prophet Muhammad. They were respected as good and wise men. The first caliph, Abu Bakr (632-634), led the conquest of Arabia. Caliph Umar (634-644) continued the conquests for Islam and led the attacks on the Persian Empire.

The Persian and Byzantine Empires

There had been civilisations in Persia for thousands of years. At the time of Muhammad, Persia was ruled by the Sassanian kings. The Byzantine Empire was once part of the great Roman Empire.

SOURCE A

Part of the ruins of the massive palace of the Kings of Persia at Ctesiphon on the River Tigris. One of the most famous Sassanian kings was Chosroes I, who ruled from 531 to 579. During his time the palace was filled with art and learning. There were beautiful mosaics and gardens.

The Byzantine cathedral of Saint Sophia was completed in 537. Its immense dome was a masterpiece of Byzantine engineering and architecture. It took only six years to build the cathedral. Saint Sophia remained a Christian cathedral until 1453 when the Muslim soldiers of the Ottoman army finally captured Constantinople. They turned the cathedral into a mosque but some of the original mosaics can still be seen.

The Byzantine capital was Constantinople. It was named after the Roman Emperor Constantine, who made it his capital in AD 324. Constantinople is now called Istanbul and is situated in modern Turkey.

Exhausted by war

Fortunately for the followers of Islam, the two empires were in a weak state by the mid-7th century.

SOURCE C

This is the view of a modern British historian.

When the Muslim attack was launched, both the Persian and Byzantine empires were in a very weak condition. They had only just emerged from a disastrous war in which the Persian Empire had been totally defeated and the Byzantine Empire completely exhausted.'

R.H.C. Davis, *A History of Medieval Europe*, 1988

The bedouin at war

Many of the Muslim fighters in the early battles were nomads. The bedouin were used to moving from place to place in search of food and water. Their way of life helped them prepare for the difficult job of moving long distances and then fighting a battle. Fighting was also a way of life to the bedouin. Tribes had a long tradition of fighting each other. When Muhammad united the tribes in the name of Islam, the bedouin tribes stopped fighting amongst themselves and made up a very powerful force. Muslims who died fighting a Jihad, or holy war, believed that they would go to paradise, or heaven.

The power of prayer

The soldiers of Islam were unlike most armies. They were united and inspired by their new religious beliefs. Every day they prayed together. During prayers they obeyed the prayer leader. This prayer leader was also the army commander whom the Muslim soldiers obeyed in battle.

> **1** Explain in your own words how praying together gave the Muslim soldiers a big advantage.
>
> **2 a** How many different reasons can you find in this unit to explain why the followers of Muhammad were so successful?
> **b** Are all these reasons of equal importance? Explain your answer.

The Battle of Qadisiya: 637

Over 1,300 years ago a battle took place between the Muslims and Persians at a place called Qadisiya. The Muslim army defeated the army of the Persian king Yezdigird. After the battle, the Muslims captured and destroyed much of the Persian capital.

Does this victory help us explain why they were able to conquer so much land so quickly?

SOURCE A

A tapestry showing events in the Battle of Qadisiya.

Catastrophe for the Persians

Look carefully at the evidence to find reasons for the Muslim victory at Qadisiya. How important do you think religious causes were in explaining why the Muslims won the Battle of Qadisiya?

SOURCE B

A modern historian's description of the Muslim and Persian armies:

'The early Arab [Muslim] warrior had no uniform. He fought in the clothes he usually wore in the desert. The Persian army was well trained. Its cavalry was mounted on fine big war horses. The Persians had a force of battle elephants trained to charge the enemy. On the back of each elephant was strapped a howdah rather like a big open box. In this were archers who fired down on the enemy.

The Persian and Muslim forces met at Qadisiya. Muslim assault parties crept under the elephants and cut the straps holding each howdah. Both sides had many casualties in the four days' battle. Those still left to fight were exhausted. But it was the Persian army which gave in.'

Adapted from V. Bailey, *Muhammad: His Time and Influence*, 1976

SOURCE C

A modern British writer describes the fighting at Qadisiya.

'The Persians outnumbered the Arab Muslims by at least two to one and had a squadron of elephants to support their infantry in the same way that tanks do in modern war. During the third day of battle large Arab reinforcements arrived from Syria.

The main problem was the elephants. Arrows shot from a distance could do little damage. No solution could be found until a few brave Arab warriors hurled their lances from close range at the elephants' eyes. The poor animals stampeded off the battlefield taking with them the Persians' only hope of victory. During the following night the advantage lay with the Arabs who split up to fight in small groups or as individuals. The next morning the Persian general, Rustam, was killed and there was little further resistance.'

P. W. Crittenden, *Islam in the Middle Ages*, 1972

A modern artist's interpretation of the Battle of Qadisiya.

SOURCE D

Naz is an Islamic teacher and writer. She described her book as 'the inspiring life story of Umar, the second caliph of Islam'.

'At last began the battle of Qadisiya. The Muslims gave three shouts of Allah-o-Akbar ("God is Great") and at the fourth plunged into operation. Once again these horrible elephants proved a great nuisance but on the second day reinforcements poured in from Syria. The troops that arrived were only 6,000 in number, but they kept pouring in, in small batches. The Persians could not gauge the Muslim strength.

One particular [Muslim] soldier fought desperately and with great success. He was a prisoner in jail for drunkenness. The man could not be held back and had pleaded with the jailer to let him go and fight as long as he returned to the cell after the day's battle was over. He fought like a tiger let loose. "By Allah! I cannot hold back a man who loves Muslims so much," said the judge when the prisoner was brought before him the next day. "By Allah set me free to fight and I will never drink again," cried the prisoner. On the third day the courage of fighters like this took the Muslims into the heart of the Persian army. The Persian king was killed. Some 30,000 Persians were beaten in the battle. The Muslim loss was only 8,000.'

Naz, *Umar the Great – a Biography of a Great Hero of the Muslim World,* 1970

---

1 What can Source A tell us about:
a Persian clothes and armour
b Persian weapons
c Persian musical instruments?

2 Look through all the sources and make a list of causes of the Muslim victory at Qadisiya.

3 a In what ways does Source D disagree with Sources B and C about the causes of the Muslim victory?

b Why do you think Source D disagrees with Sources B and C about the causes of the Muslim victory?

4 Which is the most useful source for a historian trying to find out about the Battle of Qadisiya?

5 Why do you think the Muslims were victorious at Qadisiya and many other battles of the period?

8

Baghdad: a place of power

The first four caliphs had all known Muhammad and they made the holy city of Medina their capital. As power passed into other hands, the centre of the Islamic Empire moved first to Damascus in Syria and then to Baghdad, which is the modern capital of Iraq.

By the beginning of the 9th century, Baghdad had become the largest city on earth. Why did this happen and what was the city like?

A thousand years ago the old city of Baghdad was the capital of a great Islamic empire. It was built in 762 by a powerful caliph called al-Mansur and was full of majestic buildings and fortifications. For the next two hundred years it grew to be one of the richest cities in the world. Who were the people who ruled Baghdad?

A tale of two families

In 661 Ali, the fourth caliph, was murdered. After his death the powerful Umayyad family ruled the Islamic Empire for nearly a hundred years from 661 to 750. They moved the capital of the empire from Medina to Damascus. Under their rule Damascus became one of the greatest and richest cities in the world with a magnificent mosque and a fabulous palace for the caliphs to live in. The Umayyads stopped the custom of electing the caliph. Instead they handed power from father to son, creating their own dynasty.

The Umayyad caliphs had much more luxurious lifestyles than the first four caliphs. Many Muslims felt that the Umayyads had strayed too far from the pure and simple life led by the early caliphs and believed that they should be overthrown.

A bloody banquet

Opposition to the Umayyads was led by the Abbasid family. They were descended from Muhammad's uncle, Abbas. They won support because they promised to return to the pure life of the first Muslims. They claimed that the Umayyads had seized power and were not the true leaders of Islam.

One hot night in June 750 the Abbasid general Abdullah invited eighty Umayyad leaders to dinner at his house. When the Umayyads sat down to dinner they were attacked by soldiers and hacked to death. Afterwards the servants wrapped the dead and dying bodies in carpets, while Abdullah and his supporters carried on eating their dinner!

A new city

In 762 Caliph al-Mansur founded the great Abbasid capital at Baghdad. Although at this time it was only a village, Baghdad was in a fertile land which was well supplied with water and was near the major trade routes. These advantages helped the new capital expand rapidly and to become one of the most important Islamic trading centres.

A description of old Baghdad by a modern historian.

'The round city, founded in 762 and completed – by 100,000 workers – in 766, was built in concentric circles [circles with the same centre], perfectly round. It had four gates and 360 towers.

On the outside was a ditch twenty metres wide, and a wall nine metres thick. The main wall was over thirty metres high and fourteen metres wide at the top. One section was reserved for the government and the army and closed off by a wall seventeen and a half metres high and twenty metres thick.

At the centre of the city was a vast square. Here stood the Golden Palace with its copper dome, and the Great Mosque. No one entered this central space except on foot and with orders to do so.'

Adapted from *Cambridge Illustrated History of the Middle Ages: Volume One*, 1989

● Baghdad was strongly fortified by huge walls. Sections within the city could be completely sealed off. Can you think of two different reasons why it was designed in this way?

Left *A modern artist's impression of the round city of Baghdad and* **above** *one of the four massive gates which protected Baghdad. A passage connected the outer and inner gates.*

The growth of the city

The round city grew rapidly. It was built in sections: the army were in one quarter; the palace and the Great Mosque in another; the government officials organised the empire from the area called the City of Peace and the workers who had built the city occupied another section. This part of the city also contained the industries which made some of the goods they needed, including building materials and tools. In the 9th century the city covered about 25 square miles and about half a million people lived there.

A great trading centre

Because it was placed on the junction of the great trade routes between China, the Middle East, Greece and the Mediterranean, Baghdad became one of the most important international trading centres of the world. It had its own industries producing textiles, leather, paper and other goods, but its markets contained products from many countries, and this helped bring great wealth to the Islamic capital.

Art and learning

In Baghdad, people of many nationalities and religions mixed together. It became a world centre for literature, art and learning. Its beautiful buildings were splendidly decorated with brilliantly coloured tiles and the rich fabrics and silks for which Baghdad was famous. Unfortunately, very little of the splendour of the ancient city survived the destruction which was to come.

Rich and poor

Islam teaches that all Muslims are equal, but this did not mean that there were no poor people in this fabulously wealthy city. Many of the people who had built Baghdad and those who worked in its industries could not afford to live in the centre of the city. Instead they often lived in very simple homes on the outskirts. There were poor farmers living in the countryside around the capital, and in the homes of the rich there were many slaves who had been bought from foreign traders. Their lives were very different from those of the caliphs, whose enormous wealth came from the taxation of the empire and the prosperity of Baghdad.

SOURCE B

Baghdad was one of the great trading centres of the world where items such as these could be bought and sold.

33

The wealth of the caliphs

Caliph Muqtadir (908-932) had 15,000 slaves. The wealth of the Abbasids can be seen in the presents the caliph gave to Byzantine ambassadors in 917. These presents included 38,000 silk curtains, 12,500 robes, 8,000 tapestries, 22,000 carpets, 1,000 horses, 4 elephants, 2 giraffes and 10,000 pieces of armour. While a few people were fantastically wealthy, most Muslims in the empire were poor.

The fall of the Abbasids

Gradually the wealth and power of the Abbasids began to be challenged. Different groups of people seized power in parts of the enormous empire. In 909, for example, the Fatimids took power in North Africa. Members of the Umayyad family, who had been defeated by the Abbasids, became the caliphs in Spain. In 1038 the Seljuk Turkish Muslims conquered lands in Iraq and Persia. The Seljuks were a warlike people who had adopted the Islamic faith. In 1055 they took control of Baghdad from the caliphs and for over 100 years they controlled much of the Islamic Empire.

1 From the information in this unit, make a timeline of the rise and fall of the Umayyad and Abbasid dynasties

2 Why did Baghdad become one of the richest and most powerful cities on earth? Give as many reasons as you can.

3 Are all the sources of equal value as evidence to the historian of old Baghdad? Explain your answer.

4 What do you think these sources tell us about the Abbasid caliphs?

Source C

The spiral minaret of the Great Mosque at Samarra, the largest mosque in Islam.

Samarra ('Happy he who sees it') was a new city founded (in Iraq) in 836 by Caliph Mutasim. There had been a rebellion against him, so he may have felt safer away from Baghdad and the major trade routes. Samarra was to be even more luxurious than Baghdad, but it was never finished and the minaret is virtually the only building left of this enormous city. The caliphs stayed at Samarra for about fifty years and then in 892 returned to Baghdad.

Source D

A miniature portrait of Harun al-Rashid. One of the most famous of the great leaders of the Abbasid Empire was the fifth caliph, Harun al-Rashid. He ruled the Abbasid Empire from 786 to 809. His ambassadors travelled far and wide and had contact with courts as far apart as France and China.

9

Change and conflict

As the power of the Abbasids decreased, the Islamic Empire began to break up. The Islamic religion remained a powerful influence but the empire was controlled by a number of rulers.

What effect did this have?

Islam: one culture or many?

During the Middle Ages the Islamic faith continued to spread and many people from different cultures became part of the Islamic world. Islam spread in different ways. In some countries it arrived with the conquering Arab Muslim soldiers. However, in much of Africa and Asia, Islam was taught by travelling traders or merchants and missionaries. The followers of Islam soon included many different people who, although linked by Islam, kept many of their own traditions.

The Crusades

The Seljuk Turks captured Baghdad in 1055 and soon they were close to Constantinople, the great centre of the Byzantine Empire. This led Pope Urban II to appeal to the West for armed support for the eastern Christians.

Palestine had been under Muslim control for over 400 years. In this time, many mosques were built and the language and customs of the Muslims were introduced. However, older traditions survived and Jews and Christians lived alongside Muslims without being forced to convert to Islam.

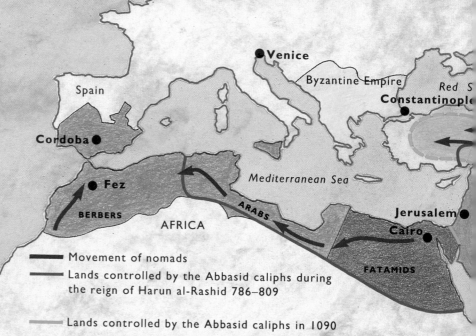

Movement of nomads

Lands controlled by the Abbasid caliphs during the reign of Harun al-Rashid 786–809

Lands controlled by the Abbasid caliphs in 1090

SOURCE A

The attack on Antioch. In June 1098 Antioch fell to the Crusaders: from William of Tyre's History, about 1280.

A divided people

By the end of the 11th century the Muslims had become divided among themselves. The Islamic Empire was no longer controlled from a single centre. Local rulers had become increasingly independent and were sometimes at war with neighbouring Muslims. This gave the Christian Crusaders the opportunity to invade successfully. In 1099 the Crusaders captured the holy city of Jerusalem. The remaining Muslim and Jewish population of the city – men, women and children – were massacred. Four Crusader states were set up and the Crusaders went on to occupy most of Palestine.

Because the Muslims were divided among themselves, they were unable for over 50 years to resist the Crusaders. However, in Saladin, the ruler of Egypt, the Muslims found a leader who was able to unite them sufficiently to recapture Jerusalem in 1187.

Although the Crusades carried on for about 200 years, there were long periods of peace. For the Christians and for Europe, the increased contact with Islam brought many lasting benefits in mathematics, commerce and trade, exploration, science and learning.

The Mongol invasion

In the 13th century, while the Crusades were still going on, a far more devastating invasion took place. The Mongol army swept into the Middle East from Central Asia bringing death and destruction wherever it went. In 1258 they captured and destroyed Baghdad. Eventually their advance into Muslim lands was halted in 1260 at the Battle of Ain Jalut. After this battle Islam continued to spread but it was over 150 years before the Ottomans created a mighty new empire which controlled much of the Islamic world.

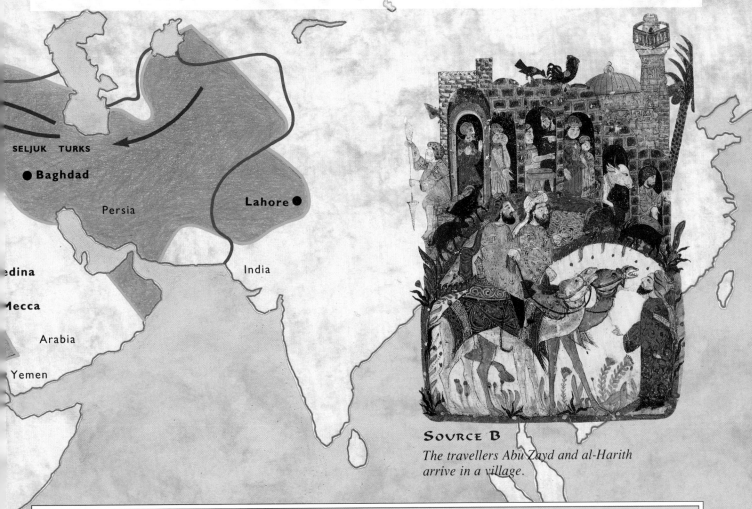

SELJUK TURKS

● Baghdad

Persia

Lahore ●

edina

India

Mecca

Arabia

Yemen

SOURCE B
The travellers Abu Zayd and al-Harith arrive in a village.

---

1 How many reasons can you find to explain why the Islamic world broke into lots of different states during the Middle Ages?

2 'Islam changed dramatically during the Middle Ages?' Would you agree with this statement.

10

The Ottoman Empire

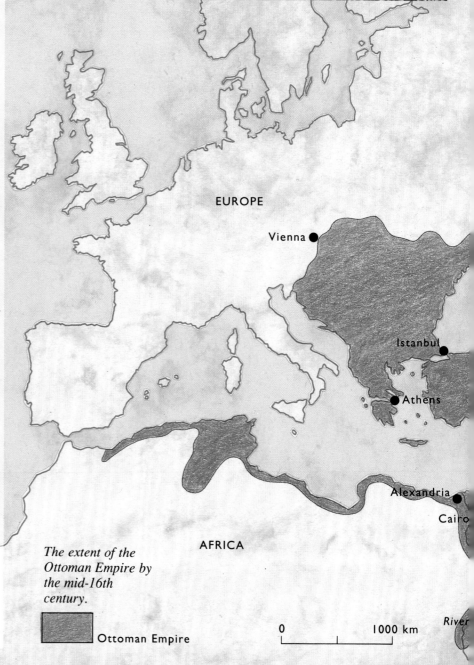

In the late Middle Ages a large part of the Islamic world was controlled by the Ottoman family. In 1453 the Ottomans captured Constantinople, capital of the Byzantine Empire.

Why were the Ottomans so successful?

The Ottoman family

In your study of medieval Britain you have learnt about the Black Death, a terrible plague which swept through Europe in 1348. Can you imagine a family which began conquering land in the century *before* the Black Death, and yet was still ruling a large empire when some of your great-grandparents were alive in the early 20th century?

This remarkable family was called the Ottomans. They were Muslims and their empire can be seen in the map. The Ottomans were Turkish.

The Ottomans capture Constantinople: 1453

The Ottoman Empire began in the 13th century, when a Turkish nomad chief called Osman fought many battles and captured land in Anatolia in modern Turkey. Two hundred years later, the capture of Constantinople brought to an end the Byzantine Empire.

- Why do you think many civilisations thought that Constantinople was an important place to have a city?

- Why do you think Christian Europe was worried when Constantinople was captured by the Ottomans?

EUROPE

Vienna

Istanbul

Athens

Alexandria

Cairo

AFRICA

The extent of the Ottoman Empire by the mid-16th century.

Ottoman Empire

0   1000 km

River

The sultan

The head of the Ottoman family was called the sultan and he ruled the empire. The Ottomans believed that the sultan's power came from God. The sultan expected absolute loyalty from his army, his officials and his people. All the land belonged to the sultan. He was the law-maker and the imam, or religious leader. However, the sultan could not just do what he liked. He had to follow the Islamic law of the Shariah. He was also the military leader. It needed a very special person to run such a huge empire.

● How does the work of a sultan compare with that of a king in medieval Britain?

Suleiman the Magnificent

Suleiman the Magnificent was a powerful sultan who ruled from 1520 to 1566.

He was not only a great soldier but also a scholar and a poet. He was a skilled goldsmith too. He had many roads, bridges, mosques and palaces built. He extended the Topkapi Palace and ordered the building of the great Suleimaniye complex of mosque, hospital, schools, and other buildings. He collected huge amounts of treasure from trade and from his many travels.

SOURCE A

Suleiman the Magnificent receiving his vassal, or subject, in Transylvania. How is Suleiman shown to be powerful?

SOURCE B

Saint Sophia: from cathedral to mosque

When the Ottomans conquered the Byzantine capital, they were amazed by the massive cathedral of Saint Sophia and its great dome (see page 27).

The Ottomans turned the cathedral into a mosque. They built minarets outside and. inside, mosaics were plastered over and replaced with inscriptions from the Quran. Today it is possible to see some of the surviving Byzantine mosaics in Saint Sophia, which is now a museum.

The army

The Ottoman army won many great victories. Its most famous troops were called the *Janissaries*. These men were taken as boys from Christian families in the empire, and trained as Muslim soldiers. During the reign of Suleiman the Magnificent there were nearly 14,000 of these Janissaries. They were carefully chosen.

- Why is a well-disciplined army a great advantage to a government?

The training of the Janissaries

Christian boys who were to become Janissaries were taken from their parents by the government. They worked in the fields for two or three years without pay. During this time they were taught the Muslim religion, and were then sent to Istanbul. Then the youths were given tough military training.

They lived in military barracks and elected their officers. They took orders only from the sultan. Their loyalty helped win many battles, but if the sultan was not a good leader he risked being overthrown by the Janissaries.

SOURCE D

A diplomat from Austria who visited an Ottoman army camp compares the Ottoman army with the Christian armies.

'They are ready for fighting. They are used to hard work. Our side is weakened, spirits broken, not enough training. Our soldiers do not obey orders, our officers are greedy and there is drunkenness. Worst of all, they are used to winning and we are used to losing.

The Turks take care to keep their soldiers in good health and protected from the weather. There is no quarrelling or violence of any kind. You never see any drinking or gambling, which is such a serious problem amongst our soldiers.'

From *The letters of Ogier de Busbecq*, the Austrian ambassador to the Ottoman court in Istanbul. 1554-1562.

Laws and taxes

Suleiman the Magnificent fought wars, but he was also a very busy law-maker. These are some of the laws he introduced:

♦ Soldiers on the march are not allowed to 'live off the land' (take food from the farmers and villagers). They have to pay for their food.

♦ Taxes will be set according to the amount people can afford to pay.

♦ People are not to be put in jail without trial.

♦ Government officials are to be chosen on how good they are at their jobs, and not on who their friends are.

♦ Judges have to be very well trained.

---

1 What information is there in this unit to show that Ottoman sultans were very powerful?

2 Some people think that Suleiman was a great leader. Others think that he was very cruel.
a Look through this unit and produce a table with these two headings:
Evidence of cruelty
Evidence of great leadership.
b Why do you think people disagree about Suleiman?

Islamic civilisation

Architecture

Many beautiful buildings throughout the world were built by Muslims or show their influence. The Islamic style of arched windows and doors influenced the appearance of many medieval buildings in western Europe. This Gothic style can be seen in many cathedrals today.

Language and literature

Many words made their way from the Islamic world into the English language. In the 15th century many old Islamic stories were collected together and now we call them The Arabian Nights. This is where famous characters like Sinbad and Aladdin come from and they have become part of our storytelling tradition.

Learning and education

Muslims built schools, universities and libraries all over their empire which attracted scholars from many countries. Important Greek books which had been lost to the West were translated into Arabic and eventually influenced the development of ideas in the western world.

and its influence

Science and mathematics

Arabic numbers replaced Roman numerals and this altered the modern appearance of mathematics. The Islamic governments encouraged and supported astronomers and scientists. Their knowledge and discoveries greatly benefited the development of science and technology throughout the world.

Trade and travel

Islamic traders carried knowledge, inventions and skills to the distant lands they visited. The inventions of Islamic scientists, such as the astrolabe, supported exploration. Map-making and a knowledge of the geography of the world increased rapidly at this time.

Medicine and hygiene

Islamic attitudes towards hygiene promoted health. Muslim doctors developed their ideas of medicine from the knowledge of the Greeks. They had hospitals and used medicines and antiseptics at a time when some westerners still depended on superstitious practices.

From the Taj Mahal to Timbuktu

We can investigate the similarities and differences in various parts of the Islamic world by looking in more detail at Islamic buildings in two countries: the Taj Mahal in Agra, India, and the mosques of Jingereber and Mopti in Mali in West Africa.

What can we learn from studying the Islamic architecture of these different lands?

A monument to a queen

The Taj Mahal was built between 1632 and 1654 as a monument to Mumtaz, Mahal wife of the Emperor Shah Jahan. There are stories that many workers died while building it, and that Shah Jahan blinded the man who designed it so that he would never create anything more beautiful. It was made out of white marble and was built next to a river and surrounded by a glorious garden.

SOURCE A

The entrance to the shrine of the Taj Mahal. Verses from the Quran decorate the entrance.

Who was the dead queen?

The Emperor Shah Jahan and his queen Mumtaz Mahal lived in luxury at the court in Agra. But in 1631 Mumtaz died suddenly, giving birth to her fourteenth child. The emperor was devastated and for a long time he was in deep mourning. In 1632 he ordered work to be started on this splendid tomb.

Respect for the dead

Muhammad did not want Muslims to build tombs in memory of the dead. Building expensive tombs went against the Muslim belief that everyone is equal in death. Yet tombs were built all over the Islamic world in places as far apart as Egypt, Iran and India. The tradition of building tombs was already very strong in the lands that the Muslims conquered.

Source B
Miniature of Mumtaz Mahal

Source C
The Taj Mahal, Agra, India, has been described as the most beautiful building in the world. It is not a mosque. It is actually a tomb built by the Emperor Shah Jahan to show his love for his dead wife, Mumtaz Mahal.

45

SOURCE D

The mosque of Jingereber, Mali. It was founded in 1325 by Mansa Musa, a ruler of Mali, after he had been on a pilgrimage to Mecca.

Mali, West Africa

Parts of Mali are covered by the Sahara Desert. The local craftspeople made most buildings out of locally available materials such as baked mud. The mosques at Mopti and Jingereber were built in this way and inside they are decorated in a simple style.

Mansa Musa was an extremely rich man, his wealth coming from the large amounts of gold which were to be found in Mali. Timbuktu became a very important trading centre, with merchants arriving there from across the Sahara. In Mansa Musa's day there were many great buildings in Timbuktu.

SOURCE E

We learn something about the wealth, power and ideas of Mansa Musa from this description of his pilgrimage to Mecca.

'Mansa Musa was an upright, godly and devout Sultan. His rule stretched far from Mali and many people from surrounding lands obeyed him. Among the signs of his goodness are that he used to free a slave every day, that he made the pilgimage to Mecca and that he built the great mosque of Timbuktu as well as many other mosques.

When he reached Mecca he wanted some of the religious leaders there to return with him to Mali. To encourage them to come he offered them huge amounts of gold.'

From Mahmud Kaatibin al-Haj al Mutawakkil Kati, *Pilgrimage of Mansa Musa*, 1325

SOURCE F

The Mopti mosque in Mali.

Beautiful gardens

As well as wonderful buildings, Muslims also created beautiful gardens. They are very important to Muslims because they not only provide water and shade, they also represent paradise on earth. The Quran mentions the ideal garden, with water, shade and beautiful flowers and fruits. The Islamic idea of an ideal garden was probably influenced by the tradition of the ancient Persians. For hundreds of years before the 7th century, the Persians had built beautiful and symmetrical gardens with pools, canals and shady fruit-trees and flowers.

SOURCE G

Look at this part of the Quran and see how heaven is described.

'The good people will be surrounded by gardens and rivers.'

The Quran (Surah 54)

SOURCE H

Muslim writers have commented on the Quran. Abdullah Yusuf Ali explains why gardens were so important to Muslims.

'In all Muslim languages the word Jannat (Garden) means Heaven. For the eye there is the green of the plants, the beauty of the rivers. For the ear there is the music of the birds, the music of the waterfalls. For the smell there is the perfume of the flowers. For the taste and touch there are the fruits.'

The Holy Quran, Commentary by Abdullah Yusuf Ali

- Why do you think water was such an important feature in the ideal garden?

- What features of the ideal Islamic garden can you see in Source I? What features were influenced by the ancient Persians?

SOURCE I

Babur, the first Mughal Emperor of India (1526-1530). He is shown giving instructions to his gardeners.

---

1 Copy and complete this chart to compare the Taj Mahal, India, with the mosque of Jingereber, Mali.

Taj Mahal	Jingereber
a	
b	
c	
d	

a What is it?
b Who ordered it to be built?
c What is it made of?
d After what event was it built?

2 Compare the mosque of Jingereber (Source D) with the Mopti mosque (Source F).
a In what ways are they similar?
b What reasons can you give for this?

3 Although the Taj Mahal and the mosque of Jingereber are both Islamic buildings they are also different in many ways. Make a list of the reasons for the similarities and differences.

4 Which building more closely follows the teaching of Islam: the mosque of Jingereber or the Taj Mahal? Give reasons for your answer.

12

The art of calligraphy

In much Islamic art we do not see pictures of people or animals. Instead we see beautiful designs based on Arabic handwriting or calligraphy.

Why was calligraphy such an important art in Islam?

The art of writing

Calligraphy is the art of beautiful writing. Ever since the Quran was first written down, Muslims have felt it an honour to copy it in handwriting. Sayings of the Prophet and quotations from the Quran have been used to decorate lots of different objects in the Islamic world, such as buildings, tiles, plates and bowls.

Muslims were also masters of geometric designs and arabesques. Patterns like those in the sources can be found on many items such as carpets, tiles, textiles, tombs and books. They can be found all over the Islamic lands.

Endless pattern

If you think back to the story of Muhammad you may remember that he taught against the worship of idols or statues. Only God should be worshipped. Muslims believe that God is everywhere and He is the creator of everything. Islamic art tries to show this belief.

SOURCE A

Traditional calligraphs are simple writings in decorative styles. Sometimes the calligraphs are made in the shape of animals, birds or human beings. The translation of this bird-shaped calligraph is: 'In the name of God, the most compassionate, the most merciful.'

SOURCE B

A Quran decorated with calligraphy.

SOURCE C

This interior view of part of the Topkapi Palace in Istanbul shows the decorative use of pattern and calligraphy.

SOURCE D

'Angels will not enter a house containing a dog or pictures. Aisha bought a cushion on which there were pictures. When the apostle of God saw them he stood at the door and would not enter. He said, "The makers of these pictures will be punished on the day of resurrection." If you must paint, then paint trees and objects that do not have a spirit in them.'

Sayings of the Prophet Muhammad from the Hadith

---

1 Read Source D. Why do Muslims teach against the drawing of humans and animals, especially in mosques?

2 Look at Source C.
a How has this building been decorated? Describe the patterns.

3 In pairs or groups design your own Islamic patterns.

13

Fighting dirt and disease

Medical knowledge in much of the world was very poor in the Middle Ages. The Islamic lands were different. Under the caliphs much medical progress was made.

How can we explain the success of Islamic health and hygiene?

A love of learning

The lands of Islam have a long tradition of education and scientific research. The caliphs built different types of schools in the conquered lands. According to Benjamin of Tudela, who died in 1173, there were twenty schools in Alexandria in Egypt. Great cities such as Cairo, Baghdad and Cordoba had universities with libraries, laboratories and observatories. The caliphs encouraged scholars from the Persian and Byzantine empires to work in these new centres of learning. The scientific works of ancient Greek writers like Aristotle and Galen were translated into Arabic.

The work of Islamic writers

The Muslims did not just copy ideas from old books. They added important new ideas. Al-Razi, for example, practised medicine in Baghdad for fifty years. He lived from 850 to 932 and wrote books about chemistry, history, medicine and other subjects. He did scientific experiments to test out the ideas of the ancient Greeks and to present medical treatments of his own. He was the first author known to have written a book about children's diseases. He also made important discoveries about smallpox.

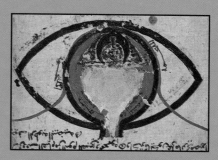

SOURCE A

A 12th-century miniature showing the anatomy of the eye and eye diseases, drawn by the Muslim miniaturist al-Mutadibi.

Understanding the human body

Al-Razi wrote a book on anatomy – the study of parts of the body. The Muslim religion, like other religions, did not allow people to cut up the human body, so there were limits to what scientists knew about the body. The most famous surgeon of the Arab world was Abul Qasim (Albucasis) of Cordoba, who died in about 1007. He designed new surgical tools and wrote an important textbook which surgeons continued to use for hundreds of years.

Mother well

Cross-section of a qanat – *a system of bringing underground water to the places where it is needed.*

Shafts

Canal

Water channel

Aquifer

Impermeable layer

Rock

SOURCE B

One of the large waterwheels or norias, *at Hama, in Syria. The water raised by the wheel flowed along the aqueduct to the left of it.*

Building dams and canals

In many of the lands of Islam water is scarce and precious. Scientists invented clever ways of saving water and transporting it for farming and for people to drink. These ideas were made possible by strong government support.

SOURCE C

Ahmad al-Hassan is a historian of Islamic technology.

'Managing a large irrigation system was a huge job. It was controlled by a government department which employed officials, engineers, inspectors, skilled workmen and labourers. The department built and maintained canals, dams and water-raising machines. Water was carefully shared out between farmers. When a new canal was approved the cost was carefully worked out against the number of hours of work done.'

Ahmad Y. al-Hassan, *Islamic Technology*, 1986

Keeping clean

You will remember from studying the Romans how good they were at providing clean water for drinking and washing. This was also important to the Islamic rulers of the Middle Ages: cleanliness is a requirement laid down in the Quran.

SOURCE D

We can find clues about Islamic ideas on health and cleanliness by looking at some of the sayings of the Prophet Muhammad.

* Cleanliness is half of faith.
* Keep your houses and yards tidy.
* Each Muslim must take regular baths and wash all of his body.
* God will not bless a nation which does not protect the rights of the weak.

Sayings of the Prophet Muhammad from the Hadith

1 How do we know that the caliphs were keen on education?

2 Why were ancient Greek writings important for Islamic students?

3 How do we know that Muslims thought that a fresh water supply was important?

4 'The Middle Ages were a time of dirt and ignorance.' Do you agree?

14

Science and stars

In important areas of knowledge, such as astronomy and mathematics, Muslim thinkers made great progress.

Why did Muslim scientists make so many important discoveries?

ROMAN NUMBERS	Arabic numbers	European numbers
		0
I	١	1
IV	٢	2
III	٣	3
IV	٤	4
V	٥	5
V I	٦	6
VII	٧	7
VIII	٨	8
IX	٩	9
X	١٠	10

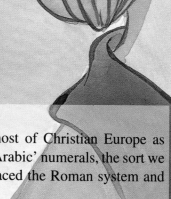

Trade and mathematics

Many important ideas and developments have come to us through Muslim scientists. The most important is probably the introduction of Arabic numerals but algebra, trigonometry and geometry were all developed by Muslim mathematicians.

Under the Umayyad and Abbasid caliphs Islam spread to parts of Africa, Europe and Asia. Traders travelled huge distances and took their ideas as well as their trading goods with them. Arabic ideas about mathematics may have been brought to the West in this way. The Romans had also brought a way of counting to the countries they conquered. It was still being used throughout most of Christian Europe as late as the 13th century. 'Arabic' numerals, the sort we use today, gradually replaced the Roman system and changed mathematics.

The numbers 1 to 9 had been in use for a long time in India. Arabs had traded with India and we know that the Muslim religion spread to India. This new way of counting was brought back to the Arab world in about the 8th century. Arabs added one more number – the zero. You may be able to see why this made a big difference.

Muslim scientists used Pythagoras' ideas to work out the distance between the earth and the moon. Muslims had good reasons for wanting to calculate distances and directions exactly. Muslims everywhere needed to know in which direction to turn for prayers and which route to take for pilgrimage. Muslim scientists could now work out these things more exactly.

Historians have studied the part played by government. This is taken from a history book written by a Muslim professor from Syria.

'Islamic rulers often had a policy encouraging science and technology. This led to the translation of books and the setting up of observatories, libraries and university mosques. Governments paid the wages of scientists and paid for research.'

Ahmad Y. al-Hassan, *Islamic Technology*, 1986

Egypt: a centre of learning

The study of science was especially strong in Egypt between 900 and 1200. The palace in Cairo had a large library and held meetings for scientists, doctors, mathematicians, astronomers, lawyers and others. Lecturers were employed to teach scientific subjects. The public were allowed in free and were given ink, pens and paper. All large mosques had libraries attached to them.

SOURCE B
A scene from an Islamic library, 13th century.

1 Explain how the following factors helped Muslim scientists:
a Trade
b The teachings of the Quran
c Using other people's ideas
d Government policy

Astronomy

Observatories for studying stars were common in parts of the Muslim lands. Muslim astronomers knew about the work of ancient Greek scientists.

Muslims used an instrument called a kamal to calculate the altitude of the Pole Star, from which they could also calculate latitude. Sailors used this method as an aid to navigation.

2 Which do you think was the most important reason why Muslim scientists were able to make important discoveries? Explain your answer.

SOURCE C
A 16th-century miniature showing Taqi al-Din and other astronomers in his observatory in Istanbul.

15 Trade and travel

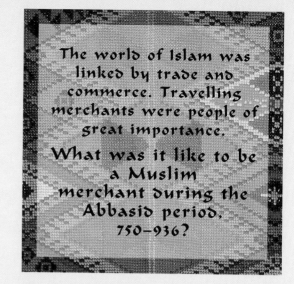

The world of Islam was linked by trade and commerce. Travelling merchants were people of great importance.

What was it like to be a Muslim merchant during the Abbasid period, 750–936?

Trade routes

The Islamic lands contained many great towns and cities. These towns traded with each other and some merchants became very rich. The map shows that Muslim trade routes covered huge distances over land and sea.

Islamic coins have been found all over Europe – even as far north as the Viking lands and Russia. Money changers were to be found in most Muslim markets. Cheques were used to make trade work more smoothly. It was said that a cheque could be written in Baghdad and cashed in Morocco. Look at the map and you will see how far apart these places were.

People in India, China, Africa and other places visited by merchants had their own ideas and customs. Sometimes the Arab traders borrowed or added to the ideas of the people they traded with.

Muslim trade routes during the Abbasid period, 750–936.

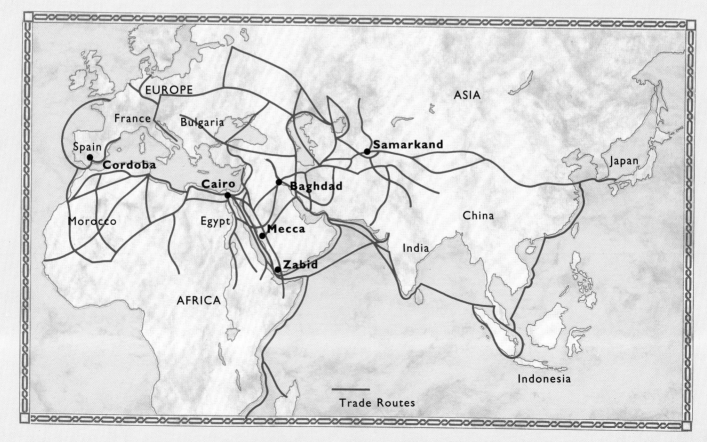

Trade Routes

A 19th-century engraving of a place where camel caravans stopped overnight. These places were sometimes built at an oasis in the desert. Sometimes a town would grow up around the stopping point, which was known as a caravanserai.

TRADING GOODS

These are some of the many products brought into Baghdad from different parts of the world by Abbasid merchants.

♦ Swords, slaves, spices, ivory and teak from India

♦ Weapons from Afghanistan

♦ Furs from Siberia

♦ Horses, pottery, silk and paper from China

♦ Slaves from Bulgaria

♦ Horses from Arabia

♦ Papyrus and linen from Egypt

♦ Wool and carpets from Armenia

♦ Slaves from East Africa.

War and peace

Although Muslims fought against Christians in the Crusades (beginning in 1095), this did not stop links between the two civilisations. For example, Christian scholars came to the great centres of learning in Islamic Spain, such as Cordoba, and returned home with Islamic ideas. We have seen that Muslims had translated ancient Greek books and had made new discoveries. These ideas helped Christian scientists in Europe.

Charles Singer is a modern historian who has looked at how technology developed in different parts of the world. He said that to some Muslim traders Europe was just a small and not very important area of land on the end of Africa and Asia. In the period from 500 to 1500 the best technology in the West came from the East. The West brought very little technology to the East.

Difficulties in travel

The traders often travelled huge distances and faced many problems and dangers. They produced some clever solutions to these problems.

Difficulties in travel

The traders often travelled huge distances and faced many problems and dangers. They produced some clever solutions to these problems.

SOURCE B

A modern historian describes one of the problems faced by Muslim traders.

'A trader's "guide book", titled "An Account of India and China", was written by the merchant Sulayman in 851. It reminds the reader to avoid the pirate-infested coasts of Baluchistan and Sind. Muslim ships arrived after a three month voyage at the port of Canton. The purpose of the voyage was to fetch back rare and expensive goods like aloes, teak, porcelain, camphor, brazil wood and tin.'

H. Bresc and P. Guichard, *The World of the Abbasids*, 1989

SOURCE C

An astrolabe was used by Muslims to find the direction of Mecca. Sailors from Europe found that it worked much better than some of their navigational instruments, and took it on voyages.

SOURCE D

An Arab dhow was useful for both short and long journeys. Its triangular 'lateen' sails were helpful for sailing in calm seas.

SOURCE E

Ibn Hawqal was a Muslim trader and traveller from Baghdad. Here he describes how he helped other traders and travellers.

'I have described the breadth and length of the earth, and I have made the Muslim provinces known. Each place is accompanied by a map showing its position. I have shown the boundaries of each region, their towns and districts, the rivers which flow through them, their surface features etc.'

From *The Travels of Ibn Hawqal*, 9th century

1 How did traders in the Islamic world help to spread new ideas?

2 Using all the sources make a list of the problems faced by Islamic traders.

3 In what ways do you think medieval trade was similar to and different from modern world trade?

Islam today

This book has been about the first thousand years of Islam. The religion remains a very powerful force in the modern world.

How can the ideas given in this book about Islam in the past help us to understand the place of Islam in the world today?

Islamic nations

There are no longer any great Islamic empires as there were in the time of the caliphs and sultans. Instead there are many independent Muslim countries. These are often very different from each other. The history of Islam which you have been studying has shown you the great changes which have taken place over a period of time but there is also continuity in the beliefs and practices of Muslims today.

The strength of belief

The Muslims gathering to pray in this British mosque could come from all over the world and represent different races and cultures. Today the majority of Muslims are not Arabs. They believe that Islam is not just a religion for 7th-century Arabia but for all humankind in all ages.

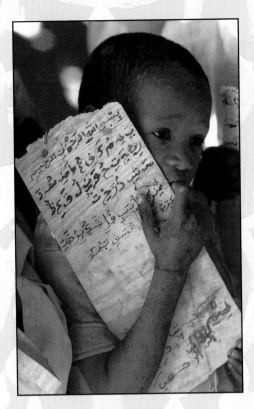

Wealth and poverty

In the Middle Ages Muslims were great traders. Some Muslim countries today have become very rich because they have discovered oil in their land which they can sell to the rest of the world. Saudi Arabia has become a very wealthy country as you can see from this picture of Riyadh, its capital, while the child seen here holding a copy of the Quran lives in Mali, one of the poorest countries in the world.

Islamic culture

This mosque, which was built in 1979, is a mixture of old and new styles.

From earliest times Islam has had a strong tradition of culture and learning. This tradition continues today. In areas such as music, literature and architecture many Muslims try to mix traditional Islamic styles with newer ideas. Today, Muslim countries and the influence of Islam continue to evolve.

Attainment target grid

This grid is designed to indicate the varying emphases on attainment targets in the questions in each unit. It is not to be interpreted as a rigid framework, but as a simple device to help the teacher plan the study unit.

✗   some focus
✗✗   strong focus
✗✗✗ main focus

		AT1 a	AT1 b	AT1 c	AT2	AT3
1	What do Muslims believe?		XX	XXX		
2	Pilgrimage to Mecca	XXX				
3	The spread of Islam	XX	XXX			
4	Arabia at the time of Muhammad		XX	XXX		
5	Muhammad and the early converts	XX		XXX		
6	The collapse of the old empires		XXX			
7	The Battle of Qadisiya: 637		X			XXX
8	Baghdad: a place of power	X	XX			XXX
9	Change and conflict	XXX	XX			
10	The Ottoman Empire				XXX	XX
11	From the Taj Mahal to Timbuktu		X	XXX		XX
12	The art of calligraphy					XXX
13	Fighting dirt and disease		XXX	X		XX
14	Science and stars		XXX			
15	Trade and travel	XXX	X			X

Attainment target focus

Activities on page 13
1 AT1c Levels 4—6
2 AT1b Levels 2—4

Activities on page 17
1 AT1a Levels 3—4
2 AT1a Levels 2—6

Activities on page 20
1 AT1a Level 3
2 AT1a Levels 3—4
3 AT1b Levels 2,3,6

Activities on page 23
1 AT1c Level 4
2 AT1c Level 4
3 AT1b Level 3

Activities on page 25
1 AT1a Levels 2—4
2 AT1c Levels 4—7

Activities on page 27
1 AT1b Level 3
2 AT1b Levels 3—6

Activities on page 29
1 AT3 Level 3
2 AT3 Levels 3—4
3 AT3 Levels 3,4,7
4 AT3 Levels 5—6
5 AT1b Level 3

Activities on page 34
1 AT1a Level 2
2 AT1b Levels 3—6
3 AT3 Levels 5—6
4 AT3 Levels 3—4

Activities on page 37
1 AT1b Levels 3—4
2 AT1a Levels 3—4

Activities on page 41
1 AT3 Levels 3—4
2 AT2 Levels 4,6

Activities on page 47
1 AT1b Level 3
  AT1c Level 4
2 AT3 Levels 3—4
3 AT1c Levels 3—6
4 AT1c Levels 3—6

Activities on page 49
1 AT3 Level 3
2 AT3 Level 3

Activities on page 51
1 AT1b Level 3
2 AT1b Level 3
3 AT3 Levels 3—4
4 AT1c Level 4

Activities on page 54
1 AT1b Levels 3—4
2 AT1b Level 6

Activities on page 59
1 AT1b Levels 3—4
2 AT3 Levels 3—4
3 AT1a Levels 3,4,6

Index